I0840975

GOD USES THE FLAWED

Repent for Wonder and Awe

by Karen Kellock Ph.D.

A new theory in psychology. According to Koestler, all landmark theories are presented in picture-strip format (right-left integration) to bring on the "aha" experience of the formula (the characteristic of all new paradigms).

FORMULA FOR THEORY:

ALL SUCCESS ATTRACTION
ALL DISEASE OBSTRUCTION
ALL RECOVERY ELIMINATION

The three obstructions are:
people, habit and food.

Remove your obstruction and
you snap to your goals,
waiting in the wings

GOD USES THE FLAWED

Self unforgiveness is a demonic stronghold holding you down/why you feel inferior to all around.   You're stuck in a hog pen when you can't forgive yourself: must shake shame/guilt to get unstuck.   When life is cluttered with negative history you never move into destiny. But self-forgiveness blocks that lie and gives you God's superpower, aye.   You can't shame a person who has forgiven himself. His history informs him by escaping hell.

ELECT ENVY

PEOPLE ARE THE PROBLEM
JEALOUSY THE MAIN PROBLEM
GOD'S OUR CHAMPION NOT MAN
PLAYING WITH FIRE
GOD'S CHOSEN: THE ELECT
THEY TAKE THE MORAL HIGHGROUND
THEY WANT WHAT YOU HAVE
IMPROVE YOURSELF TO WIN
WICKED BANDS: STICKY
TWO WORLDS
PURITY THE KEY TO GOD'S ENERGY
DEEPLY MEANINGFUL SOLITUDE
OVERCOME CRUTCHES
PERSEVERE TO ADAPT
YOU TRIGGER ENVY
SET APART AND HATED
THE INCAPACITY FOR LEISURE
QUALITY CHOCOLATEER
CHOCOLATE RESPECT
FINDING THE CACAO LINE
CACAO THE BEAUTY DIET
HEADACHES WILL GO AWAY

ELECT ENVY

Embracing self-acceptance means accepting all aspects of self including FLAWS real or false.

The most important thing in advancing our viewpoint and energies is to protect our boundaries.

The chosen can't stand being around groups of people. Due to great sensitivity it's very explainable.

Just by being different they saw you in a dark light but now pure you're in a class by yourself, aye.

PEOPLE ARE THE PROBLEM

As the block to success, people are the problem! If only we could see this, instead we let em all in.

Isolation saved your life. I know it's hard to realize being alone all the time but it's God's way, aye.

Like Joseph's brothers they're angry at you for getting more--God's reward-- and that means war.

Many had to relocate because they came into wealth and their friends were jealous, hatefully felt.

Since you were called to be set apart you can't blend in with the world. To deep empaths it's torture.

JEALOUSY THE MAIN PROBLEM

Now knowing jealousy to be the biggest human emotion you're equipped to move amongst them.

Narcissists are known to incite jealousy but that's a dangerous place to be especially presently.

ELECT ENVY

God rewards His kids and they're hated for it. That's the gist of it: knowing it makes you equipped.

It was easy for them to jump on the bandwagon against you, now they gotta pay thru a bad mood.

GOD'S OUR CHAMPION NOT MAN

God is about to show you off chosen one. He's kept you a work in progress— until now you were hidden.

They thought they were gonna get away with it Scot free but an angry God was my Champion see.

You did nothing to them but they were cold blooded and you know it. It's always the jealousy juggernaut.

God is your Champion but He's removed Himself from them cuz they chose the other side hon'.

You gave em second and third chances and they came against you anyway. I'm telling you, stay away.

They're trying to bring you down cuz Satan in them hates God in you and that's not endin' Sue.

Many foes lose spouse first so they see what it was like when you were alone and by them cursed.

PLAYING WITH FIRE

Touch Not My Anointed: there, the bible clearly says it. He'll be your champion and they will perish.

A little voice inside em said to stop going but they said "hell with that, I'll have fun getting back."

If a person values himself then his time as more important than other people [he's seen as evil].

ELECT ENVY

If one values himself then his time is more important than other people [could be seen as evil].

When you're immature & undeveloped the world flows in: unboundaried it was YOU not them.

If they don't value your time they're not treating you right cuz they don't value their own, aye.

The New Agers were time-wasters because it was more important to kissup/hangout with y'all.

They attacked me with derision for being alone not a hangout but who cares, they're locked out.

The pretty socials waste so much time socializing, palliating, mollifying and faction balancing see.

The problem is after going separate they live in your head. All the time, what you shoulda said.

GOD'S CHOSEN: THE ELECT

Elect envy is all about them trying to get to you and you resisting/learning how to manage em too.

You can't help that everyone's staring, you're a chosen and that means higher energy but modestly.

What they wanted for you will now happen to them. Every failed plan will fall back on their head.

Jealousy is the problem. There's bound to be envy since God rewards His family in clear view of the enemy.

Genius life is in two stages: preparatory and success [enjoying/reaping, usually after relocating].

Don't tell me to be nice. Help me to maintain my solitude while safely managing the mice.

ELECT ENVY

You think those little creeps/your old network will allow you privacy/time to cross that great divide?

You think the neighborhood will ever stop talking or for old misdeeds forgiving? Never entirely see.

There was always a subtle devaluation you could FEEL, making you hold on tighter: it was unreal.

THEY TAKE THE MORAL HIGHGROUND

Or she'd take the moral highground in order to trigger an argument to put you down: ah, women.

Or she'd bring up something in order to grandstand with you seen as moral scum then go mum.

Even after relocating you'll be reacting in your new territory for that's how PTSD is processing.

Once boundaried you can't believe looking back when you were like a sieve: so very dangerous sis.

It was so absurd/outlandish what they did when YOU let em in. Put the onus on yourself to forget em.

If you value time you use it to improve yourself and make for better living: who needs people then?

People are the problem cuz even after relocatin' they're still in your head and you're still reactin'.

THEY WANT WHAT YOU HAVE

They want what you have so much, they're not gonna stay away unless you construct a wall Mary.

I let em all in, "no walls" I said. Then I was robbed, looted, insulted and invaded by their friends.

ELECT ENVY

If you need someone else to make you feel better you're not in the right frame of mind, a loser.

You need a team who puts in the same amount of energy as you. If they don't, fire/remove.

No more begging them to work. When you see that smerk remove yourself/don't fight the jerk.

You've perfected/invented your technique and working full time it seems. Now just cruise the scene.

IMPROVE YOURSELF TO WIN

The more time to improving yourself the less they can play with you and you're more interesting too.

To think how you were devalued by her narrow mind! You took it on, begged and groveled, aye.

The more unique you become the less time you'll have for them then you're finally free of scum.

Your old network could even get violent when you separate so that's why I say: relocate.

They expected to keep using you and when the supply was withheld anything could happen fool.

If properly relocated it's unlikely losers will follow you, they stay local looking for others to use.

WICKED BANDS: STICKY

People are sticky: these are wicked bands between you and them. Cut these loose for freedom.

So you don't get any attention at all. This is due to being hidden under God's hand until you're called.

ELECT ENVY

If they find you act like you don't know them. You're in a new era with a spiritual right to reinvention.

Get good at saying goodbye--become an expert at it! See it as a right and a clearing for success.

TWO WORLDS

The extreme contrast between shallow conversations and deep thoughts can be very jarring son.

In solitude we can explore the inner worlds without distraction. It's for reflection not retreat son.

Solitude is the only defense against this constant barrage of misunderstandings of the elect.

Why risk being rejected or misunderstood? It's easier to retreat away from those hearts of wood.

A crowd of shallow relationships won't satisfy our need for connection like the ordinary people man.

The empath searches for equal intensity and depth only to be met with disappointment instead.

It's not easy when you refuse to compromise your principals or dilute your message at all.

As warriors for truth they must be steadfast in the face of adversity and that requires God's energy.

PURITY THE KEY TO GOD'S ENERGY

The key to God's energy is purity and sin will make it all fall down into history's forgotten gutter see.

They don't like me talking about man's sins. They want abstruse concepts-- anything other than.

ELECT ENVY

But sin is something we all must conquer. It's being the true warrior: over self then onto the world sir.

If God's elect--the chosen ones--don't purify they're the WORST OF THE LOT I've heard it said, aye.

They told me and ancestors: don't drink or you'll end in the gutter not your destiny as a great orator.

For SIN is the whole issue: Jesus first said REPENT YE. It's so basic only His death atoned for thee.

The Elect are human and must confront their own demons so there are inner/outer obstructions.

No friends they can trust, demons inside causing ruckus, a resilient life that feels precarious.

Alcoholism is not just a once in awhile beer, it's going off on a toot and dying in the gutter: Satan's lure.

The solitary path is difficult but deeply meaningful as it contributes to the evolution of humanity all.

DEEPLY MEANINGFUL SOLITUDE

The awakening of collective consciousness is triggered by ONE: a charismatic figure has now sprung.

They divert from mainstream culture and societal norms. I'd been out in the wilderness, alone.

Their unique perspective, values and energies set em apart from the crowd of vapid ordinaries.

They feel like outsiders in a world prioritizing conformity and sameness: youth make a big thing of this.

If we don't adapt and conform they see us as inferior not a mind designed to trigger change [superior].

ELECT ENVY

We try to blend in but never shake the feeling of our differences and of not quite belonging sis.

Chosen ones see the world thru a different lens challenging convention and tired wisdom.

I played the role of elf on the edge of town or professor who didn't like you coming around.

What I learned is real belonging comes from within in honoring our true selves and convictions.

Driven to seek meaning/fulfillment beyond the confines of everyday existence they may seek drugs.

OVERCOME CRUTCHES

Just more obstacles to overcome, releasing crutches of all kinds to reveal divinity in the inner realm.

We are constantly pulled to our higher purpose like a beacon guiding us and you all know this.

Solitude is not just a preference but a strategic choice in service of our higher purpose for God sis.

We have more need for such crutches than others since we don't fit/feel illegit-
-the biggest instigator.

To cultivate our inner landscapes and dive deep into our true being sounds mystical but is a real thing.

Self-acceptance is crucial for chosen: by honoring their super-sensitivity to energies all around.

Your sensitivities are not a weakness but a profound gift to the world sis. Your isolation is the door to it.

You see the world in ways the others do not. Harness it to transform the mob, your mission from God.

ELECT ENVY

We felt bombarded by expectations, projections and pressures from others and escaped soon after.

The worst were false churches. They pressured for conformity & said we hated God if we didn't.

PERSEVERE TO ADAPT

It's a giant change from eggs and bacon to chocolate so give your poor body a chance to adjust.

Soon you will see your skin, so much better/younger and softer. This gives you faith to go further.

The iridescent beauty of the skin is assurance enough you're on the right path to healthy revolution.

While mornings are high-energy errand-filled creative whirlwinds, lunch is nutritious calm me down.

Your marvelous body instrument adapts to any diet. Give it a chance to show superiority: go for it.

After being hyper-creative all night long and busy all mornin' we nap in the aft after luncheon.

SAY NO FOR EMOTIONAL BALANCE

We maintain our emotional balance by saying NO when necessary and having no qualms about it see.

The combo of saying NO while prioritizing self-care is the answer to happy life from now on dear.

Have a healthy respect for chocolate: eat too much and get sick. In the same way, avoid the hicks.

Anything that wants to drag you outa your home when you wanna stay--avoid that guy right away.

ELECT ENVY

He says "it'll do you good" when only you know what soothes your tired soul being so misunderstood.

You don't wanna do this/don't wanna do that. Now be FIRM and stay home, unpressured by that rat.

Cultivating inner strength [to stave off] is our ongoing practice. It must be or we'd go mad sis.

We build resilience in the face of adversity and peace amongst chaos: now we can exist as boss.

Building this citadel of self-belief allows us to navigate the world with confidence, but it takes guts.

YOU TRIGGER ENVY

A house built on strong traditions can't stand a new belief challenging all they've known.

The presence of a chosen one is like a wrecking ball to societal norms, thus he's threatened with harm.

Chosen one: you shake things up, causing discomfort. Don't block it, lift up your voice as a trumpet.

Why they hate: People are threatened by change and heavily invested in all they've arranged.

If God Himself chose you, do you really think you can get along with some joker in Satan's crew?

Men who didn't even deserve a conversation you felt in love with due to low self-esteem/estimation.

And then as these jokers tore you down you regressed into female clown or drunkard in town.

He loved you when UP not who you were after he used you up and you started begging nonstop.

ELECT ENVY

I know what you've been thru and I was friggin' there too when God saved me from the utterly cruel.

SET APART AND HATED

Your very presence pisses them off. It's a spiritual thing and that idea alone should relieve you a lot.

They hate what they don't understand and that's been the problem since the beginning of man.

Fear of change/transformation is a powerful force. Our instinct is to push back challengers of course.

Isolation is the one sure way to human happiness [Glenn Gould]. I see this too, it's like making gold.

You're set apart by qualities making you special and In some cases you're even seen as a rascal.

THE DEEP HURT MORE

The deep hurt more, there's no way of changing that sir: we have more to endure than ever before.

They hurt more cuz they can't explain it on top of it. Until they resolve it they're maladaptants.

So that was life: terror on all sides. The adversary's arrogant & makes us feel small as he derides.

Since then I've come to a safe place and reasonable state: people so different without that hate.

You can prevent damage from exposure to them no more than enter a gas chamber without harm.

Just because you understand a problem doesn't mean you can expose yourself to it unbitten.

ELECT ENVY

Enter a room and be instantly caught up with all the interlocking vibrations of kin down on luck.

The time is late and you've had a lot of pain in your life from hate. Time to retire and enjoy it all ok?

Understand this people and plan carefully or you can be suddenly broken without remedy.

You know how fast life can change, you've experienced sudden upsets--that's wisdom of the aged.

Like driving defensively, you conger all that can happen and after weighing things make your decision.

They hate what they don't understand and women are worse when it comes to novelty disdain.

THE INCAPACITY FOR LEISURE

Realize when tired and it's time to stop. Now its relaxation which is how you keep creativity up.

Leisure: For our days are in two speeds, as is the week: we work then we relax and we alternate it see.

Would-be genius has an incapacity for leisure. It's very important or a work becomes dull: horrors.

Two days no acid reflux, headaches or racing heart. I've now mastered chocolate for the day's start.

QUALITY CHOCOLATEER

I feel really good, much better than bacon and eggs. You gotta master it tho': wisdoms of the age.

Eat chocolate: now you're packed with magnesium, potassium and many other good things ma'am.

ELECT ENVY

Quality organic dark chocolate is far more nutritious than all that produce in the stores, see this.

Lacto-Fruitarian Choclatarian. Breakfast bar then red salad with cheese for luncheon: heaven!

Occasionally steamed with garlic butter: mushrooms and yellow squash [a fruit] or whatever.

But basically I want the raw crunch of red bells with romaine lettuce and cheese: what a thrill.

After a delicious red Greek salad take no more chocolate lest you wanna be up all night kid.

If you wanna have a steak have at it--it's not part of my matrix and I don't know why I avoid it.

Eating little bits of chocolate acts as a vaccine so you can eat larger amounts without any pain.

HEADACHES WILL GO AWAY

I was amazed: my headaches went away in a day. My system said "hello" & cacao was the way.

After flying high all night into the morning you should be exhausted by noon. Eat then fast [swoon}.

You see little improvements [even if just colon eliminations] and know you'll go on with it.

Anything that improves your good looks that much has gotta be dynamite for your health as such.

Workaholics [driven to succeed due to past lunatics] can't stop work like this so practice it sis.

Bad early life explanation: All sin even in blindness has a consequence and you were not yet woken.

ELECT ENVY

You're blue then someone calls and you're alright again Sue but you should be happy alone too.

Democrats revealed their priorities and it's not you or your family, It's about them and power only.

Work hard, and then having done your work you can just be yourself with no need to butter people up.

GOD USES THE FLAWED
Repent for Wonder and Awe

SELF-FORGIVENESS FOR SUCCESS
FORGIVE SELF OR SUCCUMB TO WORLD
THE PAST BRINGS YOU TO DESTINY
GUILT = SETTLING FOR SOUL TIES
PAUL IS THE GREATEST EXAMPLE
WEAPONIZING THE MOB: FASCISM
FASCISM: THE GODLESS GROUP
NARCISSIST OR ZVENGALI
RASPUTIN ARCHETYPE AND THE QUEEN
QUEEN NEEDS ONLY HERSELF
NARCISSISTIC CHARM AND WIT
REVEALED WITH TIME
SOLITUDE IS ADDICTIVE
BORING MEETINGS OR GENIUS
HARD TO GET PRIVACY TO WORK
WORLD GOES STRANGELY DIM
COLLEGE WAS A FOG
JESUS SAID NO ONE'S GOOD
NARCISSISTS DO SELFISH THINGS
FAME IS TERRIFYING
BLACK CLOUD FROM LIBERAL SLOGANS
YOUR PEOPLE SCARED ME
DE-FOCUS FROM SUDDEN SUCCESSES
I WAS A GRASSHOPPER IN HIS EYES
COLLABORATOR TRASH
HELL IS WHERE THERE IS NO REASON
IN YOUR FACE ABOUT IT
LIBS CREATE MIS-PERCEPTIONS
WE HAVE NOTHING IN COMMON

GOD USES THE FLAWED

Repent for Wonder and Awe

SAVE ME THE TROUBLE, LEAVE MR. EXPENDIBLE
LIBERALS ARE COMMUNIST
SAVE YOUR ENERGY, STAY DETACHED
I'M SICK OF EM AND YOU SHOULD BE TOO
TRUMP WANTS OUR FREEDOM!
MULTITUDES OF FALSE FEMALE ACCUSERS
NEVER TAKE THE BAIT AGAIN
IT'S SO EMBARRASSING YOU THINK SHE'S GREAT
EGO DRIVEN AND POWER MAD
LAUGHTER WITH STEEL COLD GAZE
LYING DEAF AND DUMB VIRTUE SIGNALERS
LIBERALS ARGUED WITH EVERYTHING WE SAID
NO PAYGAP BUT THEY WON'T SEE THAT
FORTY YEARS OF LIBERAL INTRANSIGIENCE/ARROGANCE
IMMORAL COMMON CORE STINKS
AMERICANS WANT COMPETENCE, NOT QUOTAS!
YOU NEVER WIN BY CONDONING SIN
TOTAL COLLAPSE OF FAÇADE/THANK YOU GOD
WATCH EM CLEAN IT ALL UP NOW
ELECTIONS AND THEIR CONSEQUENCES
WATCH FENCE SITTERS
STAY ON POINT, DON'T GET DRAWN IN
OUR GUY WON, GET OVER IT
DELICIOUS VINDICATION: OUR WAY IS BEST
POPULISM = AMERICANA = RENAISSANCE
FALSE ACCUSATIONS NEVER STOP SO IGNORE IT ALL
SIGN OF TYRANNY: IN YOUR FACE ABOUT IT
FIRST HE'S INSANE THEN THEY AGREE
WHITE ELDER FEMINISTS RUIN US
THE FAST

GOD USES THE FLAWED

Repent for Wonder and Awe

SELF-FORGIVENESS FOR SUCCESS

The inability to forgive yourself is a demonic stronghold keeping the best of you buried/getting old.

It's called Victim Blame. If skirt's too short and you're raped, if a showy car and you're robbed.

I went thru all that to write about it, I have to believe that otherwise life seems empty/dystopic.

She ruined her husband's life but that's the nature of the beast: not knowing what she's doing.

The nieces/nephews [flying monkeys of the narcissist] are not guilt free, to hell with all of thee.

I became such a purist I was embarrassed to be human and that's when I felt I made a wrong turn.

Self unforgiveness is a demonic stronghold holding you down, why you feel inferior to all around.

Gain: I did that but I choose to take the lesson and wisdom from it not the pain and the shame.

FORGIVE SELF OR SUCCUMB TO WORLD

Self-forgiveness takes away the world's power over your life and gives you God's superpower, aye.

GOD USES THE FLAWED

You can't shame a person who has forgiven himself. His history informs him, his destiny it benefits.

Stuck in a hogpen because you can't forgive yourself. Must shake shame & guilt to get unstuck.

To forgive yourself you pack up your past, put it away and then make room for a new season.

As long as your life is cluttered with negative history you will never move into your destiny.

When preoccupied with past failures we're unprepared for the winds of change ready to blow ok.

When God swoops in to take you to a new season but you haven't fully packed up the past son.

Making a space: the principal of pneumaticity. New life can comes in while before it stayed empty.

The divine directive is: forgive yourself and get on with the rest of your life or stay in misery, aye.

What you see today was hiding beneath the surface of my dysfunction: staying back, unforgiven.

God said regarding self-forgiveness: "you are not your failures and they don't define you sis."

THE PAST BRINGS YOU TO DESTINY

I will use everything you've gone thru to bring you to the place I've predestined for you. God

I must forgive myself to the point I don't care what they say anymore. It is only the Lord.

You did it, it wasn't right. But how long to persecute yourself for experiences making you wise?

GOD USES THE FLAWED

When we forgive ourselves we empty out the the guilt holding us captive to a dead past: dust.

He breaks the bondage of his current situation by forgiving himself then the father could too.

Memories create guilt, a debilitating mindset paralyzing him into the condition he needs to change.

Many times guilt prevents the breaking of a soul tie. Sex creates guilt then suddenly you're stuck, aye.

You know you're better than that but sinking to a low point it's horrifying/you can't believe it.

The guilt is like waist deep quicksand. It won't kill you but won't allow you to move forward man.

GUILT = SETTLING FOR SOUL TIES

Subconsciously she settles for the soul tie since guilt makes her feel unworthy of a good guy.

Stuck in a soul tie you can't empty the guilt blocking you from seeing yourself as morally built.

Unworthy of anything better she settles for that dumb fella who just wants to use Cinderella.

Paul's drastic change came from his ability to forgive himself. He could even being a murderer, hell.

Paul had crucified and killed people using the name of Christ but became a great apostle, aye.

From all the things he had done against the church he had become the international voice of her.

Forgetting those things behind while reaching for those things before: that is the highest calling sir.

GOD USES THE FLAWED

Paul says he put to rest everything in the past and reached forward without shame at last.

PAUL IS THE GREATEST EXAMPLE

He wouldn't allow the fact he fell for this or allowed that, he pressed forward to what God had.

They can't move forward without seeing themselves differently. Without self-love = no changing.

When God changed the fallen heart of man He did it with love. We have to learn to love us.

You not forgiving won't stop me forgiving myself. I won't be held captive to guilt, I want growth.

This self-forgiveness is the opportunity to redefine ourselves which is totally prevented otherwise.

We can't change or move forward without seeing us differently on the inside, empowered.

Holding yourself to former failures you never see yourself differently and life's just an ugly mirror.

No matter what you did just let it go or stay where you are: a stuck/slow self-hater from long ago.

Most people forgive self based on how others forgive them but Jesus gives a fresh slate, amen.

1. Forgive yourself. 2. Move forward with your life. God's already forgiven you so can go high.

WEAPONIZING THE MOB: FASCISM

When they lack a relationship with God they inevitably band together outa fear: the angry mob.

GOD USES THE FLAWED

Submitting to a straw man for a tiny taste of dominance they become just a beast in the jungle mass. [

Fascism is the weaponization of the mob mentality: a band of sticks with a hatchet on top see.

On the family level the narcissist excites the mob [the flying monkey members] to abuse the odd.

Under the direction of the narcissist the mob becomes a lunatic and the monkeys do the dirty work.

Flying monkeys seem naive but concur with the ring leader behind the scene: they're guilty.

The flying monkeys are the workers--the basis of fascism as you felt in family members.

It's a secret conspiracy and the victim can feel it but is labeled paranoid psychotic/even medicated.

Ask any genius: it's always the mob. All thru history it attacked the odd/those connected to God.

It's always an agreed-upon conspiracy of everyone in the family going mute when he's around see.

Fascists [weaklings banned together under a straw man] are the weakest spiritually among us.

FASCISM: THE GODLESS GROUP

Fascism is godlessness and it always involves the evil crowd [mobism] and it's lowered intelligence.

Fascis [Latin]: sticks bound together to form a deadly weapon. It's also the sick family system.

The all-inclusive mob mentality in the family is why we go no-contact: to stamp it out completely.

GOD USES THE FLAWED

You flying monkeys love submitting to the straw man for a small taste of dominance, you know that.

Spiritually speaking the fascis are the weakest among us yet we're allowing them to destroy us.

When they say they don't know what a woman is they're heiling the New World Order [the wokers].

NARCISSIST OR ZVENGALI

It hurts to see self for first time. It's the negredo stage of making gold: no one's as bad as me, aye.

Luckily most of your crutches were hidden and besides they always saw the genius of the situation.

Ok you were a weirdo, junkie or whatever. It was a mal-adaptation to the dumbed Dunning-Kruger.

How else to fit into the insane world created by social engineers after WWII like multi-genders.

People without boundaries should scare you honey. You lay em, they bust em--that's the warning.

A narcissist takes over and makes all the decisions so that fits right in with a submissive woman.

RASPUTIN ARCHETYPE AND THE QUEEN

Doesn't matter how high up she is. Recall Queen of Russia and Rasputin--instantly she was his.

He knows it, and she knows it. No word need be spoken, she's totally into his dominion.

She instantly recognizes strength/true power and everyone else pales in significance for sure.

GOD USES THE FLAWED

And she falls into his web. This can happen no matter what the man's station in life, it's a bet.

It's not a Zvengali relationship for it's not based on her low self-esteem but them as a team.

Honey what else can you do but act right. Life's a bitch and will bite you in the butt/easily ignite.

I did it again. When not knowing it or even when I did it was traumatic bad association/misled.

It feels like an exciting, powerful spirit but actually it's sluggish--within a short while you're onto it.

He was my Rasputin--a very dangerous fellow hon'--until I saw his lousy work ethic/bedlam.

He was Rasputin--woulda done anything for him--until i saw his laziness doing what he's promisin'.

Rasputin was a cloud without rain and so are you again, gotta see through images or it's your shame.

QUEEN NEEDS ONLY HERSELF

She's gotta get over thinking she needs him to complete. Just do it sister, he's a cheat.

It's their work ethic separating good from the bad. Learn to see thru images with this cad.

They talk a good game but never deliver. You begin to realize this because you're clear as a faster.

You soon see their empty bag of tricks/broken promises ain't it and you're again free of twits.

If the child is terrified and traumatized it grows into paranoid ideations as an adult, aye.

GOD USES THE FLAWED

The narcissist may be super-sensitive/intelligent as he walls off emotions too profound for him.

The narcissist will do anything to not feel those deep emotions as a reaction to abuse early on.

Delayed grieving for momma: multiple losses, poor social support, stress and a history of trauma.

\Delayed grieving for momma morphed into my soul desire to be alone and not imposed on.

Self judgment takes over as the inner critic--the sadistic superego--swoops in to justify or not feel.

NARCISSISTIC CHARM AND WIT

The supersensitive grief stricken narcissist learns charm and wit can stave off emotions/self-regulate.

Their charm and appeal is short-lived and that is the difference in the narcissistic defense: glib.

They can be excellent conversationalists making you feel centermost but then later you're toast.

They make you feel like a prized person to know then you see it's just a set up/attack from below.

What utter disappointments these energy thieves bring on. You've gotta be ready, learn and go on.

Without a skill set the already traumatized one will continue to spiral down/the fall is profound.

Wrong decisions made in a fallen state of mind affect decades to come and that's narcissism.

Without any self-awareness every act is to wall off feelings of the facts, we're out of grace.

GOD USES THE FLAWED

They can't keep it up: their supposed interest in you. Their entitlement always reveals itself too.

With time your uniquenesses or other interests show up and they become a lot less fluffy nonstop.

With time, what you owe them becomes more of a centerpiece and you feel obligated again.

Good character as opposed to superficiality requires time to cultivate/they don't have it mate.

REVEALED WITH TIME

With time, what you owe them becomes the whole centerpiece and you feel pain without cease.

The crumbling of the helpful personna: if you don't face it as a trauma you may fall to the bottom.

Stay away, keep em out. This is the era of the sociopathic narcissists running all around.

With time he may go away on his own as what YOU want you make known. Pray to be alone.

Pray he'll leave and never come back. Dream of how you'll feel independent of this dreaded flack.

If he was good for you you wouldn't feel this way. Pray for release so you can enjoy THIS very day.

He's a haunted house of demons about to slither away because you again asked to have your way.

He'll be gone before you know it cuz you asked God your Father to eliminate the fake/horrid.

This was the last indicator of an early trauma & what I chose on the outside to duplicate momma.

GOD USES THE FLAWED

If they come off as "too ideal" while you see they can't manage/refuse the real, he's a slippery eel.

Your uniqueness will raise its ugly head and you will see the end result: he's gone, thank God.

You can't trust anyone in small liberal town cuz it's all about virtue signaling or being drugged.

Everyone who came to the door seemed like a voracious animal, a big fat fish and social criminal.

SOLITUDE IS ADDICTIVE

Solitude is so peaceful it becomes addictive. People drain your energy immediately and you feel it.

No news is as important as just going inside and listening to your heart. NONE, nil, don't even start.

Around em I feel instantly drained. I'm so peculiar I feel I have to explain as on my parade they rain.

It's a sucking spirit I sense: that they're stealing my soul right outa me and they want all I have, see?

Sucking spirits wanna take all you own and your soul too. It uses you up/spits you out/makes you blue.

I felt the sucking spirit when two neighbor kids came over. They wanted everything, it's like an odor.

The sucking spirit is communist: it wants what you have, greedy with desire tho' denies being materialist.

A most sickening subset of the sucking spirit is the borrowers. Don't lend stuff out/keep order.

They always wanna borrow stuff. Make em get their own--these people are nothingness, ridiculous, fluff.

GOD USES THE FLAWED

BORING MEETINGS OR GENIUS

The Mormons gotta partake in boring meetings not do something important for mankind as a genius.

If I wanna fill my home with nice things that's my right. I don't have to share it, that's not "the light".

It's all ego coming up with these things. The mental mind can easily go wrong, it's about your premises.

The major premises--like "we are one"--determines the subsets, the finer details of just being dumb.

I'd get into trouble for saying "these people". But they were a rabble/sick as the devil--the social.

They demanded I go to boring meetings not stay home & do my work--just to make me heel the jerks.

HARD TO GET PRIVACY TO WORK

It's near impossible to get privacy to work. For a female it seems like the whole world are interrupters.

When in a family it requires spine and strength to demand privacy to work-- office hours as it were.

How can I think with you in the room? Don't you understand, silence isn't enough--vamoose.

Solitude isn't a feather in your cap [worn as monk image] but a matter of survival, please see this.

I can't take it anymore. I've suffered, written all about it and now recovering in the sun, exhausted.

The more you suffered the more you'll get back now. Men abused you so now men'll celebrate you: wow.

GOD USES THE FLAWED

As interesting as the news is, the real fascination is your own inner journey to the True Self and God.

The True Self is as God designed, every peculiar inch. It's the groove we fall into after repentance.

It's like this: Insofar as we come to God we come to our True Selves. It's entirely unique not a conformist.

It's easy to lose your mind and intelligence cuz it's MORAL IQ of the heart that is the highest.

With repentance one reward is your own unique genius coming out so forget past/get into that.

Just do your own thing and you'll be higher than a kite. Don't bring your mind down with spite.

WORLD GOES STRANGELY DIM

The world will go strangely dim the minute you get into your own thing. It's like it all flakes to nothing.

They hurt me so much with their nasty, horrible misjudgments but that's the herd sis.

It's THEM with the dirty minds but they're projecting it all onto you. The pure prince/lady is screwed.

I've been thru all this, I know. I'm in safety now and it's heaven on earth to be protected by a wall.

His sickening treachery hurt my gut. I can even feel it now: every night my pillow was tear soaked.

My body fell apart living in a treacherous environment of ruthless disdain, gossip and jealousy triangles.

You must ring a bell with them--strike a chord, trigger an unconscious analogy, bring insight/revelation.

GOD USES THE FLAWED

When someone you trusted turns like that on cheap bribes or just being a rat it's scary as heck.

I'm still sore about all those people you brought over. Who do you think you are--it was a disaster.

If they're so social and out of control like the Jersey Shore kids don't trust any of em, EVER/good riddance.

I'm still sore about you leaving your boyfriend at my house. How would you know how we mix?

Men hated me for being smart, women for being cute, older for being novel, pros for seeing home as all.

Why go to your boring meetings and get-togethers when I have my HOME, there is no comparison.

For most it's blanked out but the saints gotta re-experience the past then it's gone at last.

COLLEGE WAS A FOG

For most, college was a fog. Sexual licentiousness and the social destroyed the experience of awe.

She railed at me cuz I wasn't available socially as she demanded--like it was The Way to salvation.

Believe me, where there are no lines--the college dorms--it's all disgusting debauchery and bedlam.

Your friends were your hit men. They caused me so much destruction and you are to blame man.

They pits of confusion, haunted houses--all from the inner sexual demons from licentiousness.

JESUS SAID NO ONE'S GOOD

GOD USES THE FLAWED

Guess I'm a misanthrope but Jesus said NO one's good [only God] so get hep, it's just the truth.

Never give em an edge to take control. Don't let her move in if you can't get rid when things go wrong.

You must INSIST on privacy and make em know it's the MOST important thing so never come again.

I'm thrilled watching history docs. It's a magic transport out of modernity and it's hard knocks.

A magical environment. For me it's wind chimes, music, eternal views, pets, hotel like neatness, quiet.

The modern sitcom is shot in a messy cluttered kitchen cuz that's "reality" to them and it's disgustin'

Jesus erases sin. It's like all the black is removed from the past leaving only white: what a blast.

I was so insane I can't recall any of this but one by one the memories re-emerge and I'm embarrassed.

It's hard to believe I coulda done such crazy things but then that's me now--mature--seeing it.

NARCISSISTS DO SELFISH THINGS

You musta done crazy things too since you're a narcissist cuz when desires lead it gets ugly/selfish.

I long for that honeymoon/vacation spirit to take over when I've gone beyond a problem, amen!

For the greatest honeymoon/vacation I just wanna stay home cuz from paradise I never roam.

Crazy, insane, ridiculous, cruel things I did in a black out from ego, society, liberal feminist narratives.

GOD USES THE FLAWED

Things have gotta turn around soon. After all this work you deserve a good break so opportune.

I smart with humiliation cuz that's the past son. Unfortunately most must go thru it, no fun.

The day of humiliation/humbling breaks the crust down to expose the spirit inside, now with great shine.

Sometimes you need God-given enemies to elevate you to your highest calling. For me it was Jane.

For writing income you gotta be famous. It makes me squeamish it's so hard staying blameless.

It started in my twenties: sister spouting liberal slogans and me getting nervous at her treachery.

The loving equality slogans are terrifying to a clear mind. They can see the communist spirit, so unkind.

It MAY pay to marry the "right" man rather than the one you love, but probably not. Think this out.

FAME IS TERRIFYING

FAME: Some people crave it while others are terrified and shirk it. The public eye: you'd better be perfect.

The communist spirit: You can't have those four kittens, you gotta give me one. Share: see Stalin.

There's nothing crueler than the communist spirit and as young as kindergarten I began to fear it.

She brought this crap home from college and our family was split apart forever, a house of cards.

Fame: Some crave it others are terrified of it as the public mind turns on a dime you're loved or despised.

GOD USES THE FLAWED

Here you're nervous about what one person thinks and you're talking millions? You may just freak.

My priorities were different in my twenties all ending in public ignominy and so I fear ridicule honey.

Fame wasn't what I thought and MAN were they mean. Meaner than to a nobody cuz it's jealousy.

They could easily kill you if you're famous but you're relatively safe if they don't know your ass.

Not only did she bring this crap home from collage she acted all superior about it. I'll never forget it.

She acted so superior in her new collage knowledge we had to agree, so unprepared were we.

Add to that a shrill voice, a superior spirit and fascistic dogma and she was the newly chosen elite.

BLACK CLOUD FROM LIBERAL SLOGANS

All I know is a black cloud came over our home after she came back from college. What a bitch.

As a prolific writer I'm too dam sensitive to be around you. I pick up on spirits and your grossness too.

I'm like a sponge darnit and as long as I'm in my room with the door closed I'm happy and can revel in it.

Mom would object to the door closed. She was threatened by my independent space ya know.

Mom was threatened I just wanted to be alone. I couldn't be an inner bubble in the dysfunctional home.

Guess you could call it a self-imposed monastery. A real one I couldn't adapt to cuz it's always tyranny.

GOD USES THE FLAWED

After adapting to creeps in my home it's now the most important thing: happy homelife thru fencing.

As a prolific writer I'm grossed out easily buster so don't do that again or I'm gone forever and ever.

I feel violence in my soul. It's from living in this culture absorbing it all and the schools started the fall.

The kids i met in the 80's were violent if they didn't get their own way. Imagine how they are today.

I have independence today so people can't yell at me anymore. I've got a locked gate and door.

It may seem strange that an elder would fear these human impositions but the whole thing stays with ya.

Im friggin' grossed out quickly. There's no lines you see so an elder like me is disgusted very easily.

YOUR PEOPLE SCARED ME

Your people scared hell outa me. There's no way I wanna see em again nor anyone in your tribe, sorry.

Get outa my house you grabby greedy mouse lookin' around/opening drawers/casing the joint, get OUT.

Time goes on and the generations die out. An endless wheel so may as well accept it/party on.

No one can rise up against me like he's gonna hit me cuz I won't give him drug money, I'm locked in honey.

Whenever they say "we're here to help" you should run the other way for its a communist set up.

You can have a wonderful home but let the wrong person in and it's ruined for everybody, forlorned.

GOD USES THE FLAWED

It's not enough to do the face/neck you gotta do the decollate as she continues on like an addict.

He's just a mere mortal who's gonna die like everyone else and dogs, cats, horses. Put GOD first.

No one has the right to judge you at this point. Put focus on Jesus, people always let you down I think.

A secret mental love affair, huh? Just another part of the stream "dying" to get in, don't let it, duh.

It's always people getting you off track. That's why marriage is so healthy, it constrains all that.

The crazy, insane and cruel things that happen from feminism when combined with alcoholism.

Take one drink and in walks another entity in your soul. He takes over and you're a dumbass that's all.

Stop thinking about your exes and other petty shit. You've got audacity, wisdom, real talent.

I only need to hear the news ONCE not repeatedly in great detail. You're wasting time, go inside now.

MUSIC is my releasor. All I gotta do is turn it on and the sudden attitude adjustment is a thriller.

DE-FOCUS FROM SUDDEN SUCCESSES

De-focus from enemy's sudden successes for it's all a mirage: God puts ONE up/another down, soon.

For these are a cruel people but now it doesn't matter cuz I'm within my locked gate and it's paradisiacal.

I don't have to search out the headlines, they're in our face. Just relax into the right brain I say.

GOD USES THE FLAWED

Wake me when it's over. In the meantime I'll enjoy music cuz frankly politics has become a dam bore.

People who disagree with climate change etc. are an "existential threat to our world" so out with ya.

Censorship kills thinking, innovation and wisdom. It leads to self-censurship and not asking questions.

With censureship the mind becomes narrower, we stop creating, free inquiry [science] is impossible.

I've narrowed the news down to Newsmax, Lou Dobbs, Tucker of course and Laura/Hannity always.

As a traumatized love addict I was a pathetic wreck like a fish swimming upstream on the begging end.

Looking back there was insanity. I didn't see it at the time cuz denial saves us from what we can't take.

The mind: If someone's smart but with the wrong premise or direction, watch out it's like a Hitler son.

"I couldn't get over him" means he triggered that old broken attachment bond with mom.

I WAS A GRASSHOPPER IN HIS EYES

Due to his reaction to me I saw myself as a grasshopper for decades: self-perception works that way.

Stop thinking about petty shit like your exes and other relics--you've got your DESTINY to enjoy kid!

The traumatized tend to idolize people--a mal-adaptation to when they weren't there for you.

Let the enemy's success be not a crisis but a stepping stone to your highest--it works like that sis.

GOD USES THE FLAWED

You built him up due to your own trauma. He's really nothing, you'll suddenly see that I promise.

God uses the flawed. He used sinner Kings to accomplish great things: I hear Trump and am awed.

Though scared to death the sun shines inside, relieving us of eight years of treachery by the snide.

The anti-Trumps are mindlessly swept up by well-funded hysteria and that's what's happening in America.

Men being emotional brittle get their hearts broken and you silly women think they're mean/forsaken.

The left has fought for sexual impropriety for decades and yet suddenly are so concerned: charades.

Charade: an absurd pretense intended to create a pleasant or respectable appearance.

COLLABORATOR TRASH

Leftists who lie about everything are collaborator trash. You're gonna lose cuz you did it all for Clinton cash.

Trump's being attacked by hyenas and jackals and you won't stand for him in these battles?

Phoniest Obama speech I ever heard, sounds so forced--blah blah, cum bay yah: false dogma=lost charisma.

Can't stand to see his face, can't stand to hear him. He's the devil and his smooth glibness is sin.

Crime after crime, horror after horror: What kind of a government allows it's people to so greatly suffer?

Liberals find equivalence between a mass murderer and a man who likes pretty women/possible flirter.

GOD USES THE FLAWED

Creepy kids attack "middle class morality"--something they heard like the script "justice and equality".

The leftist's era is fading. All over we're sick of this false ideology, so immoral and degrading.

HELL IS WHERE THERE IS NO REASON

Hell is a place where there is no reason. Dante

TV heads: brains eaten.

Milo isn't conservative he's a provocateur. That's not a good thing cuz it's decency we want, you hear?

Milo is truly obscene when you listen to him. My goodness don't let children hear talk like vermin.

Milo seems like a global operative meant to sully our view of the right and it's a stink and blight.

Liberals see themselves with a self-righteous halo. But debunk their delusions and it gets personal.

Trump says "it's ok to love your country" but they're teaching us to hate our nation, land of the free.

They've been using sports to control people since ancient times. This is no different, over the line.

To hell with the globalist NFL. Dads: Stop watching it and take your kids camping--break this spell.

They say we're bad for not wanting to watch steroid heads spit on the flag every time, Trump's so right.

Every break's anti-gun, anti-family, anti-Christian. We're not gonna take this treachery anymore son.

Your bread and circuses now disgusts us.

GOD USES THE FLAWED

Conservatives like pragmatic policies that work. Liberals just wanna feel good about it (comes first).

With liberals, entitlement justifies fraud. Though wrong, their ideology seems right but it's not of God.

All I can do is the best I know how. At least I do something, not act tough like you--ducks in a row.

IN YOUR FACE ABOUT IT

It's all about rubbing our noses in it, dominating and squatting on top of us while submitting to their tyranny.

To a demoralized person, the facts mean nothing. He is unable to access true information: dumbing.

They prey on our demoralized perception as the "gospel truth" then destabilize our world/call us fools.

Obama ok'd to kill 40,000 horses. Can't you see what a monster he is threatening animals, our values, even houses?

Liberals see males through a feminist lens which is anti-men. It's unfair, brutal, false weights and offends.

We're in the middle of a culture war and the main media's on the other side and it's Trump they abhor.

What we need again is bold preaching on hell and holiness not new age nonsense creating this mess.

Money buys privacy. Like not having to rent rooms to strangers for lousy money.

The hippies promoted Ameriphobia since the sixties, now old bag Hillary keeps doing it though sickly.

Black cop shoots a black guy--it's white people's fault. With liberal trendies it's prejudice they exalt.

GOD USES THE FLAWED

The people who attack first are the bad guys and that's Antifa.

Whatever the herd does you go along with it. You gotta judge things by the bible and not ignore it.

LIBS CREATE MIS-PERCEPTIONS

Libs create the perception of an epidemic of police going after blacks to kill em--all bull hon'.

You don't hate Trump from his speeches (for he's great) you're just against him cuz the herd it pleases.

BLM given several hundred million dollars--now they're in power teaming with ISIS and other fowlers.

A sign of superiority is not bending with insults--not even flinching cuz you know it's the devil's bitching.

They were cute kids but I don't like anyone after they've gone off to school. They become cruel, called "cool".

Never forget the debate--the most important one in history as we approached the razors edge and our fate.

Effects of our collective hate is sure to take him down sometime for he's not invincible nor sublime.

Youtube has brigades of social justice warriors censuring and demonetizing until you conform.

Trump made it ok to be politically incorrect so now masses are going through that wedge: the elect!

Blacks, listen up: He didn't care about you--he gave it all to his Muslim buddies, an American tragedy.

Dangerous territory: "Fact checking" is opinion journalism pretending to be heightened objectivity.

GOD USES THE FLAWED

The arrogance of Wash D.C. will soon come face to face with the American voter--watch! Donald Trump

Has it come to this--families divided over Trump vs. all the politically correct crap? Yes, so dump.

Desperate, they do more absurd things each day. Grab your seat/watch the show and joyfully pray.

WE HAVE NOTHING IN COMMON

If you're gonna vote that way and be such a dumbass we have nothing in common and I'll be droppin.

I can be the best I can be cuz I got a man to protect me, what do you have (feminist throw-away for free)?

We've gotta stop trusting people just cuz they're cute! Look past looks cuz Lucifer is beautiful and astute.

We must confront immature kids and not let em get away with this as their deception surely increases.

Trust that it's a landmark world revolution. Trump is about protection, borders and nationalism.

They've had internet control for a week: They don't do things right away so we feel false complacency.

Our dumbness will get us as we go along with ISIS and it's the kids--that is my studied hypothesis.

It's our time to shine, or after this we'll be in decline. That's how it goes in seasons of man and bloodlines.

Paul Ryan is more upset with Donald Trump's locker room talk than the assault on America by Barack.

We reflect our generation but we gotta rise above it. It's sick as it can be with promiscuity--don't be it.

GOD USES THE FLAWED

Wow--I eliminated ten Trump-haters just today. Feels like a two ton enema getting rid of the dumb fray.

Republican war on women? That's absurd. The war is from the left leading them to hell/isolation.

The war on women is the left leading to abortion and immoral deceptions causing lost affections.

SAVE ME THE TROUBLE, LEAVE MR. EXPENDIBLE

Save me the trouble and leave (this right-wing pinnacle) on the double cause you are expendable.

All the things democrats believe in are immoral and evil. Here's a list of the goals of these crazy people.

Democrats are evil but they may not know it. That's how singed their conscience is--they even love it.

White privilege, what kinda bull is this. And so you give them all mansions and put me in the dust?

Hillary, Bill and Barack don't care because liberals in general don't care about a thing--no lines, only flings.

It's in for women to be violent with their men: Angelina Jolie and Hillary for example, time and again.

I don't care if I only have five friends left. Say something against Trump no matter what and I'll drop.

You hate Trump so what was the alternative? Hillary, tyranny, guns taken and flooded with the enemy.

Liberals are always feigning great benevolence then thieving behind the scenes. Evil helpers, fiends.

No matter who they are liberals say the same thing cuz it's a script and it's so annoying it gets us ticked.

GOD USES THE FLAWED

If you hate everyone it's cuz liberals are everywhere, mockin'--it's been the default setting since kindergarden.

My Donald prayed before the debate and that's why he was so great and never took the bait.

LIBERALS ARE COMMUNIST

Liberals are communist. They want everything equal and that means taking from you ("sharing") and it's evil.

As people reflect their generation they become morally insane. "Moral sanity": gone/decency is slain.

When you hear "Trump is losing", always think: not true. All bull. Liberal hype/stink.

A well-informed conservative is every liberal's worst nightmare. Elvin Bartley

I dis-friended fifty people, so go ahead--make my day: If you hate Trump that's all you gotta say.

Liberals are always faking great benevolence. But have you ever been betrayed by one, by chance?

Savior of USA raised up by God. Has foibles (called "odd") but when in full power we'll all be awed.

The Hillary supporters are dumb, dowdy and dangerous. They only know she's a woman (though traitorous).

In contrast to the medieval religion that chops off hands we still have faith in man's humanity to man.

Hillary doesn't care about murdering babies/dismembering abortions: she's a sleaze/moral moron.

Let those envying your thirst for power take note of your fate. You've done yourself in, with hell you've a date.

GOD USES THE FLAWED

Criminal Takeover: Crooks have been in control but soon Donald will be on a roll and save America's soul.

SAVE YOUR ENERGY, STAY DETACHED

Save your energy. Instead of getting mad at a liberal, see it's a script that they all advance (trivial).

Soon Donald will reverse things. Biblically, God shows up at the last minute to save the day. hurray!

We need R and R after eight years of terrible trauma seeing our great country dismantled by Obama.

He handled it perfectly, overcoming resistance which vaporized as his detractors were scandalized.

If woman don't "give in" they really "stand out" bringing great respect despite what he expects.

It is so nice that the shackles have been taken off me and I can now fight for America the way I want to. Donald Trump

Women's scorn, worse than men. They don't forget, comes up time and again. Warning: Don't let her in.

When women rule they can be the worst (but some are cool). We're talking war: not for fools.

I've been under liberal women and really, it was vermin and I shudder to think of it (end of sermon).

I understand frustrations of men dealing with feminists--It's always horrible as they destroy the nest.

Feminism is the default setting so it's just as hard being lady as having morals and keeping chastity.

Adapting to feminists is the worst. It's cuz they're borrowing a personality not their nature (the first).

GOD USES THE FLAWED

Don't give into creepy kids. I know how they pressure but you must stand strong and ignore their fibs.

I'M SICK OF EM AND YOU SHOULD BE TOO

I'd rather be alone for the rest of my life than ever argue with a lazy lascivious liberal again. Amen.

Adapting to liberals brings mental illness. Only the strongest can withstand it's effects I guess.

Liberals make big bucks cuz they work for the system though it sux and that's why they're arrogant: in luck.

Kids will attack your insistence on decency (no sleepovers, no locked doors) but you must missy.

The pope has endorsed Donald! This is interesting after the morality issue in this recent squabble.

As a psychologist I see no narcissism in Trump whatsoever. It's ok to be proud of your works so clever.

On Nov. 8 Wash. D.C. faces the righteous justice of the American voter and it's about time. Donald Trump

Conservatives relate to Trump on a deep cellular level--to us every word describes angels vs. devils.

Just like children they don't know the difference between right and wrong. Embarrassing, isn't it: the human throng.

A very exciting day, as Mr. Trump has taken the gloves off and I love his every word! Exhilarating! Oh my!

Christians couldn't vote for Clinton cuz she's for abortion and taking away our first amendment: no options!

Clinton would even kill newborns--that's the progressive agenda, more and more gore the Christians abhor.

GOD USES THE FLAWED

I hate to impose this on you but it's the truth about this son of a pornographer and prostitute.

TRUMP WANTS OUR FREEDOM!

Trump wants freedom. Hillary wants world government, unlimited immigration and rule by corporations.

Pat Robertson said he had a vision of Trump at the right hand of God and I believe it/don't find it odd.

Trump is a wonderful man. And you're a creep if you wanted Hillary, a horrible woman so please leave vermin.

Putin has no choice but to war against the attacks of Obama and Clinton but with Trump we'll rejoice.

It isn't freedom to free violent prisoners, it's tyranny--cuz then more control is needed, believe me.

Feminist sisters did it to my mother too: put her down for her old traditions with no respect (so cruel!)

This happened across the land when the new feminism began: your poor parents were attacked, man!

Mom was against it all (abortion, homosexuality, sexually free) and was bashed into drinking and insanity.

The selective outrage from the left about sexual impropriety is more a projection from them, entirely.

Trump's a nice family man with a love of female beauty and you equate that with that rapist, really?

See reality: If he lost she'd have won and we're dead. Study what she'd do and take note of all she said.

The leftist media are best at promoting rape hoaxes like on campus, disproven X times--just ask us.

GOD USES THE FLAWED

Leftist media is expert in concocting fake rape stories but also the expert in ignoring real ones (never sorry).

MULTITUDES OF FALSE FEMALE ACCUSERS

Multitudes of females will now accuse Donald cuz that's the left media's way (they are simply awful).

There will be multitudes of accusers now, thus dulling the impact of real rape accusations we know.

Understand people that if he loses, we're dead. Tell everyone--go ahead--for we live on the razor's edge.

Lies and deception: I don't wanna live in a divide-and-conquer system but renaissance and creation.

Every time they try this crap it blows up in their face. Out of desperation they've lost first place.

They see both as equally bad. That shows lack of morals cuz there's no comparison/we've all been had.

Angelina Jolie lost her looks which come from truth/God. No translucency, looks pasty: lackluster/odd.

Angi Jolie's face shows bloated planes. It's from spouting false dogma, not being true and underlying shame.

Hillary's America: Keep babies alive to get body parts. Dear Lord how far we've fallen into hell/dark arts.

Mainstream media's stranglehold on propaganda is just about done. They lied all along but with Trump we won.

They say Hill stinks like Obama: hell's fumes and flies. The devil is revealed in ways which we all despise.

I hate the republican party. Trump is an outlier, a dark horse taking it over and it's all for us: making it hearty.

GOD USES THE FLAWED

We broke through the mainstream media's blackout on Bill Clinton's rapes. Now we're yelling--great!

NEVER TAKE THE BAIT AGAIN

Progressives: we don't take the bait. We know what you're doing but just want you out (can't wait).

We put up with enough of that in California. People coming late or not at all-- no more of this, I warn ya.

Here in Utah man walks tall. It's Old America, so unlike the coasts where people come late/not at all.

They deliberately use rare words. No one knows the meaning--pseudo-intellectuals are for the birds.

Their penchant for using obscure terms reeks of snobbery. It's sophomoric youth doing this, really.

They're a mutual admiration society where one loser praises another: useless vain youth--why bother?

The left uses skewed polls to make their point. Don't acknowledge any of em, they disappoint.

Election Stress Disorder was killing me, knowing what I know: that if she won we'd go under tyranny.

Women want secure borders, safety, law and order. So why would they want Hillary, the welcomer?

The more human rights the less likely you'll be extracted from home (with a black bag over head) at night.

It's so embarrassing you think it's great. Have you no class, wisdom, discernment of truth vs. base?

IT'S SO EMBARRASSING YOU THINK SHE'S GREAT

—and what about your mate?

GOD USES THE FLAWED

As soon as they say they're for Hillary Clinton you know who they are so don't fight em, just forget em.

It's the most massive, epic, gangsterlike and murdering by one in recent history and she's only begun.

It wasn't the person who made us insane, it was liberalism which is so false it's a sanity-drain.

The thing about liberals is they enforce their false ideology with tyranny so get ready to be unhappy...

Resistance to tyrants is obedience to God. Thomas Jefferson

Suddenly all the anti-war activists/pacifists want war with Russia. Isn't that an interesting discussion.

EGO DRIVEN AND POWER MAD

Ego-driven and power mad. So bullyish they challenge the nationalist Putin: it's so dangerous and bad.

Seasoned warriors are against war. The world changes when you've been there/seen all the gore.

The world changes when sucker punched by the foe. You see everything differently--that's how we grow.

Ghandi said it: First they ignore you, then they laugh at you, then they attack you, then you win. Amen!

She goes out of her way to be a demon but when the camera's are on she's totally loving and even.

Why would anyone want war with Russia when they could have peace? It's the left that can't be appeased.

Rules for Radicals: Accuse your opponent of what you are guilty of. It's as simple as that but it gets rough.

GOD USES THE FLAWED

Just a little freedom and fabulous wealth is created. It works every time with lower taxes/deregulated.

Whatever she says goes. She's busy taking notes of how to get back and massive networks to hurt foes.

They vote for who they think will win. It's human nature so these fake polls sayin' she was ahead were sin.

To Hillary Clinton steadiness marks the true leader: making decisions that will kill the outsiders.

LAUGHTER WITH STEEL COLD GAZE

First she laughed. But Hillary's new persona of steel cold gaze and even hatred--what to make of it?

Revelation: As soon as she got in she'd become a male. Just to mess with our heads, make us crazy/fail.

What a bunch of bull sayin' "they're both bad". Just shut up if you're gonna be so dumb you cad.

Why women shouldn't rule nations: Either they're warmongers or they tolerate abominations.

Women taking her side last night, saying "he encroached" are just showing who they are: dumb toast.

They are clearly floundering, ramping up fake assaults on Trump each week to distract from wiki-leaks.

Not strong enough to be themselves, they slip down to the popular groove and become evil elves.

You tell by what they write they have nothing inside but sometimes they chirp a slogan and it's snide.

They compare America to utopia and say "it doesn't measure up" so create hell holes/blow everything up.

GOD USES THE FLAWED

Getting mad at every dummy you meet will take all your precious energy since they're all doublespeak.

Stop spouting off you liberal creeps. For short-term fame your career is over cuz we're the power peeps.

A Muslim dictator destroyed USA and we never protested. Now a guy wants to save us and we can't accept it?

LYING DEAF AND DUMB VIRTUE SIGNALERS

The lying deaf and dumb virtue signalers of the left: if we don't stop them it's the end of the west.

Our nation' s best and brightest have been brainwashed into our dumb and dumbest. Pamela Geller

At this time we see massive mental illness: Stockholm syndrome, confirmation bias, lying to us.

In such turbulent times Trump gives us peace of mind. He's not a smiling ineffectual wimp like the other guy.

Wholesome Americana thrives despite the vicious left. So who is God blessing--can you guess?

There's a glorification of wickedness on the left. It's so sickening--no wonder we're worn out and bereft.

Alpha isn't criminal, it stands for what's right and goes against peer pressure: that's true might.

The left hates the west, Christianity, prosperity and open/free societies.

Hillary stole but still lost. Progressives think nothing of fraud cuz their "higher goal" is worth the cost.

Election gave us gumption to blaspheme the 60's saints (Hillary) and their religion of hollow progression.

GOD USES THE FLAWED

Liberals got what they wanted (can you imagine this): we can kill our babies. That's how cold, dark, shady.

Liberals laughed at our morals, our restraint. They tried to bring us down to their level and not be saints.

LIBERALS ARGUED WITH EVERYTHING WE SAID

Liberals argued with everything we said. Their guidebook to bring us down: confuse, destroy, wreck our plans.

They rained on our parade and took the wind out of our sails. It was all so depressing walking on nails.

They always wanted to control. If unawares this was a terrible snare but resistance built muscle/let em stare.

Liberals were so smug and arrogant. They laughed in our face, they called us stupid but they were "excellent".

How can I sweep it under the rug-with-a-hug after you caused me undue pain for 8 years by being so dumb?

It's not just about Trump: The liberals have been in control of our reality for decades: dirty, base, cold.

People lost all refinement and dignity. They became dirty and even felt pride about it: easy, flirty, floozy.

I want to be part of a Renaissance not a controlled paradigm. I want creative freedom, all mine.

Trump wants to incentivize/cut taxes for the black community--oh, isn't he as horrible as he can be?

The criminality of the democrats is linked to media and the stars. Hollywood has degraded us so far.

Race pimps and crybabies are losing steam--all based on fallacy cuz things are not what they seem.

GOD USES THE FLAWED

Hillary's machine (celebs, activists, hacks) so devoted to getting her elected are shocked at the true collective.

It's tyranny (what it's been) or Renaissance (an explosion of prosperity and creativity: innovation).

NO PAYGAP BUT THEY WON'T SEE THAT

There is no pay-gap: Women are paid as much as men.

We're now in the driver's seat. So now just party on, ignore the rioters and get ready for the future, a treat.

What America is really all about: leaving people alone. It's about the individual happily on his throne.

They call us all "Russians" cuz we wanna cut taxes and we care about our veterans.

Zero taxes and major development for black areas--and they say Trump's a racist and bad for America?

Moral relativism crushed our ability to feel. We lost empathy and became selfish, debauched/would even steal.

It's so bad we can't copy any part of it. We must become Puritans-the other way--as our country began when fit.

When people lost morals they also lost excellence and many became like trash, indecent and dense.

Now we can return to true class, like when things were nice. When they were excellent, sweet spice.

The greatest part is not being bullied anymore. We've won/we're right and they're wrong: media whores.

Those 8 years were terrible: Waking up every morning with dread, fearing we'd end in a camp or dead.

GOD USES THE FLAWED

Renaissance is about flowering of the free human will. It built America but liberals want to kill it still?

Under Trump more than half won't pay taxes. Such a bad man, isn't he? The anti-Trumpists know nothing/are asses.

Hollywood scum trying to divide this country say "whites are inherently bad/racist": This is the bigotry.

FORTY YEARS OF LIBERAL INTRANSIGIENCE/ARROGANCE

It's not just about Trump but the last 40 years of being on the begging end with liberal arrogance/intransigence.

Politics has split families for 40 years--conservatives became the black sheep: alone, bewildered and in tears.

Liberals said there was nothing wrong with it. We could do it and God wouldn't have a fit: not legit.

Revive the incredible American dynamo: No taxes for working people, not letting globalists sell us out (evil).

They worship in vain, teaching as doctrines the commandments of men. math 15:9

Popularity does not determine truth--just the opposite.

Conformity to insanity, sadism and verbal abuse of the left: snap back or nature wipes you out instead.

The democratic party has never been so upset since the Republicans outlawed slavery. Alex Jones

Americana: A system so good everyone adopted it willingly. Protestors are bought/divorced from reality.

Now we've won, our real work starts: Re-educate dumbed public, teach kids Civics and warm stony hearts.

GOD USES THE FLAWED

Hollywood has lost all class. It's now a promoter of globalism and taking our guns but not theirs: the brass.

The left wants to destroy our constitution, traditions/customs. They want us busted, or to be Muslims.

They parade like they're so superior: peas in a pod. Meanwhile they bash you a learned nerd as "odd".

IMMORAL COMMON CORE STINKS

The immoral Common Core stinks--turning sweet kids into sex pots--and it's disgusting beyond belief.

Liberals breaking down into conniption fits over devastating defeat when they thought they were elite.

Why do they love disorder and collapse? Because they're the devil, absolute evil: learn the facts.

Thanksgiving saw families fighting over politics: it happens when you're frantic and they're thick as bricks.

Our dinner guest was so self-discrediting but she may not see it for several years, God be willing.

What a moral vanity trip she was on! Virtue signaling while being a moron incapable of polite conversation.

She discredited herself so thoroughly and even got drunk over it. Wow, universities: you're filled with it!

Don't you understand, he has to play the game with cards held close, ok? Their ego blinds them to the fake.

False doctrine is a filth, cancer and drought.

Obama's Whitehouse always sympathized with the killers, like thugs were his only emotional pillars.

GOD USES THE FLAWED

You have to learn to stay apart from the mess: the church is full of ravenous wolves the bible confessed.

Everything in life tries to wear us down: socially, emotionally, financially but with God, the crown.

He won't receive a thing from the Lord bcuz he's double minded and unstable in all his ways.

AMERICANS WANT COMPETENCE, NOT QUOTAS!

Americans want competence not quotas.

The more they smear him the more I made the right decision cuz they're the problem/not solution.

The easily offended: easily manipulated and will always do crazy things to be accepted, never admitting it.

They don't feel we're in danger cuz they don't get the news--only state brainwashing, without a clue.

Why America's on the wane: Left wing policies brought staggering indebtedness impossible to maintain.

Now we really see who's dumb enough to go along with the herd. It lends discernment, a great barometer.

Soon we'll be rid of the filthy, debauched and sex-centered public schools and common core making whores.

I've been there, recall Vietnam? We were self-righteously angry too, but this new thing seems a scam.

Obama's "Medal of Freedom" was given out like lollipops to all his leftist friends/supporters though dumb.

Clinton and Podesta see it as a war and in war people do get killed: no big thing blood and gore.

TV is only good for old movies. Modern movies reflect liberalism since the sixties: cheap, dirty and cheesy.

GOD USES THE FLAWED

Cry babies and dummies don't know history: Immoral, debauched, tainted, brainwashed, immature, lazy.

The freedom that creates so many fantastic opportunities is hated by the left and the globalists.

YOU NEVER WIN BY CONDONING SIN

They bought into the false paradigm 8 years ago, delusionally thinking they were winners by condoning sinners.

They are the racists: All the KKK (krazy kollege kids) see is skin color and it's very serious with these brawlers.

I think you're so shallow you liked him for his looks and style. He was "cool" so you didn't see the hostile/vile.

Nothing tastes so delicious as vindication, more than riches. It is them not us who were the evil witches.

We went through too darn much to just sweep it under the couch, calling us arrogant fascists and grouch.

The democrats want a permanent underclass.

They perverted our will and our kids. They made us accept the unacceptable so we self-medicated/lost our lids.

Liberals are indecent trash. If there's any doubt lets discuss each point and you'll see they're scum/out for cash.

They act so superior, saying "what you said was so disturbing" as if you're bad not those heartless cads.

Trump's transfer of power to the states will be transformational and that will appeal to the least rational.

Trump will face the ridicule of treachery if he doesn't put Clinton misdeeds before a grand jury.

Don't be afraid, we're going to bring your country back. Donald Trump

GOD USES THE FLAWED

Our guy is keeping all his promises and more. Under Obama state legs lost 900 dems off the floor!

It's a total collapse of a giant con artist's facade: media meltdown mania--thank you so much God!

TOTAL COLLAPSE OF FAÇADE/THANK YOU GOD

So good to have a president who's not out to get us, isn't it? He actually loves us/hard getting used to it.

Stop saying I'm racist when I'm not racist. This is getting old you creating crises so get real and fight ISIS

"Do everything we say or you're a weak-minded racist" only works with the weak not the intelligent (elite).

Obama vacations cost $100 million. That's predictable with liberals, though everyone else has to live like peons.

2nd American Revolution was bloodless and targeted the heartless--removed doubts/made us courageous.

The dictator's reign of terror is combined with his huge smile. That's how he does it, that's his style.

Obama: Fearing every day I was spied on, or taken to a FEMA camp. Fear of Martial Law, stuff like that.

Establishment discredited (it's now a huge joke) while Trump has the beachhead, having removed the yoke.

J-Z and Beyonce prostituted themselves by taking 68 mil to champion Hillary Clinton, the rotten.

Donald is a return to clarity and true intelligence. He rings a bell down deep--it's called Aesthetic Knowledge.

Obama was a daily trauma and a severe undertow as our dreams did blow away but now it's all-ok!

GOD USES THE FLAWED

I am very optimistic that Trump will fix it.

Never been so happy in my life after 8 long arduous years of daily trauma from Obama and strife.

WATCH EM CLEAN IT ALL UP NOW

Now we get to watch it all being cleaned up. The trash, filth and liberalism as we drain the swamp.

Our guy won, that's all I need to know. No need to argue with liberals anymore--no time to blow!

They'll see with time the one against gays and women was Hillary cuz she wanted to let in their enemy.

It's wonderful to respect our leader once more: We were so diminished and embarrassed by that bore!

The question is: How much trouble can Barry cause on the way out? His agenda's not done yet, wow.

This is only the beginning but at least there's a beginning not an ending as I feared days ago.

Liberals: You supported a proven criminal, a pedophile. We'll always remember how you're defiled.

Liberals: They're for women/gays--what a joke! Shallow, supported a known criminal=up in smoke.

Liberals have such poor character to support a criminal doing such bad things--now let that register.

Clean sweep. He'll repeal Obamacare Plan along with other executive orders: Trump's the fix-it man.

God turned the tables in the presence of our enemies. Haha: we're onto you now: moochers for freebies.

GOD USES THE FLAWED

Give up on liberals--Why argue with such low-info voters? We're sick of that, they've become bores.

Go easy? The hell we will--it feels too good after 4 decades of being made to accept liberal falsehoods!

ELECTIONS AND THEIR CONSEQUENCES

Elections have consequences and they will be huge. Even liberals will see when restored, prosperous and new.

I still can't listen to FOX--even in victory. I can't forget how they minimized him/were so contradictory.

I'm finding it hilarious, table-turning, relieving and educational. After all, they supported a known criminal.

I have not slept well in eight years. I was daily shocked, dismayed, enraged and many days in tears.

What does it all mean? It's so deep and electrifying to think of the implications now we've stopped dying.

No one controls like the democrats. They are the tyrants: communists under leftist cover/dirty rats.

They say "unify"--like we can forget all they put us through: censoring, bullying and banning me/you.

Oh the glorious feeling, transcending way above a problem. His name was Obama with his fold of goblins.

It's like saying "now that we've defeated Hitler (Jeffrey Donner) let's unify with him". That's leftism again.

I'm gonna party for a year. The daily trauma of adapting to liberals wore me out but now it's joy/no tears.

Anyone calling for unity has a false premise of reality. You can't unify with evil: they must repent, people!

GOD USES THE FLAWED

What happens with all the bombs, bullets and tanks in Obama's army that has built up over the land?

WATCH FENCE SITTERS

Have they changed their views on abortion or are they just jumping on the success bandwagon (again)?

Can we unify with those wanting to pervert our kids, take our guns, open the borders, ban God forever?

Have they changed views on things Christians find abhorrent? Or do they just want what's current?

To all you Hillary supporters crying in your soup: We got so tired of the corruption and the cesspool!

Their tears of unfathomable sadness are yummy today! Yep, it's corruption/cesspool for decades.

We've won, relax--get out in nature more. You're a lot tireder than you know after 8 years of horror.

If they're bitter from Hillary losing they aren't God's people. She believes in killing babies--get a grip, ladies!

God appears at the last moment to save a culture from the brink: that's His style, now we can think.

People must repent before we trust them again. Tolerance is an evil word, it brought ruin of Rome in sin.

Odors: The riots are instigated by Hillary Clinton's bed-wetting, whining, tantrum-throwing supporters.

Pity Party Mental Illness vs. Trumpism: secure borders, lower taxes, turbo-charge economy, Americana.

The left has inflicted such wickedness, hate and race-baiting garbage while blaming us for the carnage.

GOD USES THE FLAWED

We see the poor losers, we see how nasty they are. Don't like his conciliation (stay a star)!

STAY ON POINT, DON'T GET DRAWN IN

Stay on point, have no conciliation: They've been compromised (scum) so will never agree with Trump.

We are on the cusp of history, at the crossroads. We've chosen the right path and got rid of our heavy load.

Not having jobs has nothing to do with racism--but NAFTA, shipping jobs abroad, factory shut down.

Wear your Trumpgear everywhere and say "we're not racist, we want freedom and you should too", hear?

Trump is an icon of irreverent resistance to political correctness. Milo Yiannopoulos

When dems thought they'd win they said "handle losing maturely" but when they lost acted destructively.

Just enjoy the holidays and ignore the cry-babies. Come January it'll all be ok because of our guys.

They root for freedom/concede to Trump but meanwhile assemble riot operations against us chumps.

Liberal = trouble. We want real America--Christian and conservative--not your stupid bubble.

Hillary supporters said to "handle it maturely" if she won but when she lost they burn it all down for fun.

One professor described it as "one of the most shocking events in our history": see why we've lost liberty?

People who watch corrupt TV news have no idea what's going on so cut em some slack for being dumb.

GOD USES THE FLAWED

Reason no false flags before election: They all thought Hillary was going to win--fake polls did themselves in.

They act like we're supposed to sweep it under the rug! Don't cave into this and face facts about the thugs!

OUR GUY WON, GET OVER IT

Our guy won, get over it. We had to put up with your guy Obama for 8 years/ wanna forget it.

Just because I'm a woman I'm supposed to identify with a group like that? What an insult--they're all brats!

In a landslide against Barrack Obama's maniacal policies we'll have an amazing country (high quality).

Higher education is isolated, insular and liberal. Average voters aren't you know.

Barrack Obama's Great Legacy: Wanted men and women to use the bathroom together and other stormy weather.

Arrogance prevents vision so they thought they'd win. Now they gotta face their wrong ideas, premises and sin.

He only wants to help, bringing prosperity back immediately. But they hate him anyway, the psycho-needy.

We're partying for one year! Our guy won and life has returned to fun--and we can keep our guns.

Interesting domino effect as the world re-assembles around the new matrix: The Trump phenomenon

Liberals are in shock. You see, because they tell us they think they speak for us: out of touch.

Everyone acts like a gangsta. It's so revealing, no thanks sir. Anything liberal is a dirty detour.

GOD USES THE FLAWED

We must arrest and prosecute this crap: Stop saying "unify"--it's not our map! They ruined/made us mad.

DELICIOUS VINDICATION: OUR WAY IS BEST

Delicious vindication: our way is best. This ties loose ends and brings it altogether but it's hard to digest.

if you cut em some slack cuz they're black or whatever it means morality's low on your list and "they can't resist".

We're scared to death of the macabre/hellish forces they've unleashed by this but we must resist.

Establishment really thought they were better than you--pride went before their fall and I saw it in them all.

They preach peace but are the most violent. They call themselves loving but no one believes it.

Trump got in, that's all I need to know. Cuz I trust him totally to take care of our safety and the foe.

Liberalism expected us to "love everybody" even if they acted horribly and that's not Christianity.

The new time has come. The world looks different released from Obama-fear and it's so much fun!

For 8 long years when the wicked ruled the people mourned with out any R and R and life was so below par.

It's all coming out now! Every little crime/lie, injunctions that made us cry, government incursions/spies.

If the creepy feminist wants to kill babies two days before delivered, how can you possibly not hate her?

It's just liberal: the pedophile, Satanist, degenerate party of the worst of us.

Their ultimate fun is to carry on Satanic rituals in a church.

GOD USES THE FLAWED

The creepy leftists were a dark evil and insidiously influential but thankfully our guy has broken that spell.

POPULISM = AMERICANA = RENAISSANCE

Populism, Americana, Renaissance: Let's dance! True Genius.

The pen is mightier than the sword. So keep writing how much you love your president and the foe you abhor.

Obama's legacy is a bunch of spoiled brats--now we see where they're at: dumbed, trite and pat.

Obama was out to get us every day for 8 long years and he had the tanks and bullets putting us in fear.

Obama seems confused that we don't like him, hate his policies, and voted in the opposite: just obtuse?

I don't even think the kids know what they're protesting about--"racist, sexist, homophobe, bigot": not.

Liberals want the fake nice irrespective of what's really going on. It's all image: smile/never frown.

Stop seeing culprits just political forces they were weak/dumb enough to be swept into. Forgive, pooh.

FOX made me crazy too. Constant rehash, liberal balancing (not enhancing) and other distractions: I'm through.

I can get all the news here, instantly. FOX is not happy simplicity, I don't need all that worldly staticity.

Boobs, cleavages, face lifts: that's FOX news. Can't take it anymore, want my reality not the blues.

Best of my favs here: Hannity, Coulter, Savage, Jones. If it's newsworthy I'll see it so no sweat being alone.

GOD USES THE FLAWED

Trump's win: a kick in the ego-gut causing further, deeper realizations of how liberalism is nuts.

FALSE ACCUSATIONS NEVER STOP SO IGNORE IT ALL

Libs still blaming Trump for rapes. Accusers all paid by Hillary/Soros--proven-- but they still hate.

Their sub-par criminal candidate lost and we're supposed to feel sorry for these cry babies? Disgust

Not everything is about race, gender and sexual orientation.

Trump got in and the stock market's soaring as oil has been discovered in Texas: Trump loves us!

Anti-Trump fixation is just a big Hollywood mouthpiece of corporate interests who have hijacked this nation.

Anti-Trumps are crazy with fears yet it'll be zero taxes for city blacks and he's been gay-friendly for 30 years.

That's my president you're talking about creep. Hear him speak then shut your mouth or be up a creek.

Obama/Clinton policies killed hundreds of thousands, really--yet their dumbed fans call Trump a bully.

They don't care if Clinton killed or terrorized cuz they've learned words like "racist/homophobe" to despise.

Dems: dead in all states/legislatures. We're sick of debauchery, treachery, thievery, hypocrisy and letchers.

Sure they'd win, they were planning how to take our guns and restrict our liberties--all friends of Hillary's.

We're thrilled at the death spiral of the corrupt communist media and the victory of the new, so remedial!

The NFL went to hell now the NBA is on it's way.

GOD USES THE FLAWED

Both coasts are crazy. They both voted for Hillary, even the ivy League and "best schools" show stupidity.

SIGN OF TYRANNY: IN YOUR FACE ABOUT IT

Sign of tyranny: in your face about it--no hiding the clearly illogical and laughable/obvious hypocrisy.

When you account for voter fraud of dead and illegals, Trump won by 7.5 million for he's the Man of the People.

The corrupt media are so arrogant they thought they'd win putting evil Hillary there and then stealing in.

The hippy loves free will and hates the thought of a predestined high groove he should fulfill.

If you live like a pig/look like a bum what's there to love? It's a meritocracy supported from above.

Unshaven grungy men reflect the new age of free will (do what thou wilt) but we hanker for back when.

Are you made in the image of God (clean order) or the dirty disorder of the devil--looking disheveled?

Everything we do should glorify God not be separate, chaotic, cacophonous, bizarre or strangely odd.

This is a culture whose default position is: you can't talk about it.

Need retraining camps for punk youth who cause these problems: goblins, know nothings, demons.

The Trump presented by fake media (CNN, MSNBC) is not the real Trump--he's our savior, not a chump!

Trump is unifying America but media is on a war against reality, blocking him out and cause hysteria.

GOD USES THE FLAWED

Terrorism defined: Violence to further political/economic aim. From liking em the media now hates em.

FIRST HE'S INSANE THEN THEY AGREE

Last month Trump was called insane to call them bad, but now all agree--the fake "news" is just a fad.

It's hard after attack not to wish them dead but maybe we should first try forgiveness instead.

Fame: 14 million views of Antifa games: white liberals screaming at blacks calling them racist names.

Frothing mental illness not just of Antifa but the mainline left in America.

Captain America: The most ignorant uneducated leftists fighting the "nazis" in complete hysteria.

Unable to express their feelings with such a limited vocabulary they resort to filthy obscenities.

WHITE ELDER FEMINISTS RUIN US

Real troublemakers are older white female liberals ("feminists") who ruin things for the rest of us.

It's hard not to swear and cuss when frustrated by the treasonous but we must.

The videos show that 95% of arrogant crazy racist nutty people are white liberal women, no kiddin'

Never give up cuz of censoring you--fight even harder cuz we will win when traitors get their due.

Middle aged white liberal women have lost their bloody minds but even our enemies make sense at times.

It wasn't marriage that screwed me up it's marriage to a dam alcoholic and that's the truth bud.

GOD USES THE FLAWED

Having been educated by "The View" white liberal mid-aged women have become the worst, peeyuu.

It's all virtue-signaling and thinking they're good as they break down our barriers for hearts of wood.

SHOCKING: They're so elitist they don't care about what we think, feel or how we're doing.

It's a situation where only the terrified can comprehend the gravity of it but I say get away, RUN.

They push an agenda that nobody wants--that's the key--then make up stuff like we all agree.

It's not so much that they coddle criminals but they don't recognize human evil: it's "all good".

Lower the IQ, more prone to violence. Delayed gratification/self-control is high intelligence.

THE FAST

It was God's gift, a blast: He removed all hunger so I could complete my 10 day water fast.

FAST: A bad cough for 40 years and now it's gone, acid reflux so bad even water brought it on.

When the Fasting Spirit came upon me all of a sudden ten hungerless days were done: I was free.

After my ten day water fast I saw the benefits more each day. Funny how it works that way.

I coughed like Hillary Clinton, an out of control situation but after a ten day fast praise God it's gone.

1. Forgive yourself. 2. Move forward with your life. God's already forgiven so now you go high.

100 KAREN KELLOCK BOOKS

AFFINITY OR MISERY
AGELESS CORNUCOPIA
AMERICA AWAKE!
AMERICA'S DAFT ERA
ARTS OF PALEO FASTING
AUTOPHAGY ON CHEATERS
BACKSTABBING NEUROTICS
BETRAYAL TRAUMA
BOOMERS AND BROKENNESS
BOOT ON NECK
CHAMPION GUIDES
COMMIE NUTHOUSE
COMMIES
COMMUNIST SPIRIT
CONTAGION OF MADNESS
CONTAGIOUS MADNESS
CULTURE CLASH BASHED
DAFT LEFT
DAILY FASTARIAN
DAM RATS
DIVERSITY IS CRUELTY
E-RACE WHITE
EVIL FREAKS (Beyond Gross)
THE END OR A BEND?
FEMALE BULLIES AND FEMI-NAZIS
FEMALE CARNALITY
FEMALE DUMB DOWN
FEMALE POWER DRIVE
FEMINISM AND RUIN 1 & 2
FIX FOR MISFITS
FOOLS & TRAMPS
FREEDOM SPEAKING
FRENEMY ENABLER
FRENEMY LIAR
FRENEMY THIEF
FRENEMY TRAITOR
TRENEMY TYRANT
GENIUS IS HELD DOWN
GLOBALISLAM
GOD USES THE FLAWED
HAZE OF THE LATTER DAYS

KAREN KELLOCK PH.D.

M.S. Political Science, San Diego State. Ph.D. in Psychology, University of California Irvine. Postdoctoral: UCI School of Medicine, Dept. of Psychiatry [NIMH Grants]. Developed the Debris Theory of Disease, a theory of system pathology in 120 books and 22 textbooks for the general public. The theory has a general formula: All disease is obstruction, all recovery is elimination, all success is attraction. The three obstructions are people, habit and food. Remove obstruction and snap to your goals, waiting in the wings.

www.ingramcontent.com/pod-product-compliance
Lightning Source LLC
Chambersburg PA
CBHW061727250726

48657CB00002B/808